Plum

Hollie McNish is based between Cambridge
and Glasgow. She has two poetry collections – *Cherry Pie*
and *Papers* – and an album, *Versus*, which made her the first
poet to record at Abbey Road Studios, London. She has also
written a poetic memoir of parenthood, *Nobody Told Me*,
and *Offside*, a play co-written with Sabrina Mahfouz
relating the history of women in UK football.
She won the 2016 Ted Hughes Award.

Hollie McNish

Plum

PICADOR

First published 2017 by Picador
an imprint of Pan Macmillan
20 New Wharf Road, London N1 9RR
Associated companies throughout the world
www.panmacmillan.com

ISBN 978-1-5098-1576-0

1 3 5 7 9 8 6 4 2

A CIP catalogue record for this book is available from the British Library.

Printed and bound by CPI Group (UK) Ltd, Croydon, CR0 4YY

Visit **www.picador.com** to read more about all our books
and to buy them. You will also find features, author interviews and
news of any author events, and you can sign up for e-newsletters
so that you're always first to hear about our new releases.

as if a million views on YouTube
means those poems are the best . . .
if I'd shat into a bucket
I'd have ten million views instead

– Hollie McNish

for everyone in here
and out there
but especially for Aunty June
and the knitting bee

Contents

(mind)

Acknowledgements

With thanks, once again, to Becky Thomas, who, if not at the Arsenal match or checking the score discreetly on her phone at readings, has tirelessly helped bring the poems I've scribbled in confused moments onto published paper. To Don, Lucie, Rhiannon, Clara and Kish for your help in all things book-shaped. To all the lovely people I've had the pleasure to meet through poetry; whether the friends who write as well and support us all or those of you who come to the gigs and chat afterwards and make it all so lovely.

To friends and family and all loved ones in here; to mum, dad, Al, gran, gaga, aunties (hope you never read this really) and past uncles; to Tracy for the bra and general brilliance and care; to Kit for the advice and love; to Nicky, and all the little cousins; to Jodie and Caroline for having called on me so often in childhood and still; to Julie, Olly, Maddy, Jo, Rowena, Laura, Kathryn, Becky, Suzanne for allowing their teenage sexed tales and periods and advice and friend-ships in here; to Hanna too, nice to have you back a bit; to Dan, always; to Donna, sorry; to Nico, sort of; to Lj, Helen, Tammy, Vim; to Inja, then and now; to the midwives; to Little One and Glimmer and Broccoli and Hermione and Harry and Ron and Bellatrix and Volde-mort and Dumbledore and Pinkie-Pie and Rainbow Dash; to Dylan and Willoughby; to Em, Jen, Sandra; to Juliet, Vicky, Sally, Kamila; to Michael (Pedersen) and all the morning fruits; to the woman from Finland and the man who rowed to her; to whoever planted the plum trees; to all the kids (including my own) I've learnt so much from recently – apologies for having to deal with us adults on a day-to-day basis; to all the people whose names I don't know but who've inspired a poem or two in here; to the birds and bees.

(mind)

How The World Should Be

(first poem I wrote down, aged 8)

After a school litter picking-trip

Meadows yellow, brown and green.
Rainbows in the sky.
No litter on the grass or fields.
Butterflies flutter by.
River water sparkly clean.
No pollution in the air.
That's how the world should be.
So try to take more care.

DANDELIONS

(written aged 30)

For mum and your advice:
'I love you to the moon and back, Hollie
but you are no more important than a tree'

when it all seems too much
and i wonder why we're here
and i think about the sun
and i wonder why it's there
and my daughter points to space

and the emptiness upsets me
and i lament my lack of god
and i wish that one would find me
and i worry what is out there
and i wonder what the point is
and i panic about death
and i panic it's all pointless
and i wonder when space stops
and what the fuck we're on this rock for

i think of strawberries in the summer
firmed and ripe and juicy
and how perfectly dandelion seeds
are made to helicopter breezes
procreating across fields

and i remind myself
this is not all about you, hollie

LOVE

Mum held out her palm that day. Runner-bean seeds. I was about
eight years old and my brother ten. Mum marked us a small patch
of soil each and we shoved our index fingers poke by poke into
the dirt, dropping one seed into each hollow. We danced across
the garden, watering cans tumbling. We waited impatiently.
We made the seed sachets into flags, sellotaped to lolly sticks.
We labelled them in our best writing. Then we stood back,
triumphant as our own moon-landing marks.

Each day after school we ran out to watch, as ever so slowly
sprouts crept through the soil. Mum stuck in a gigantic wooden
pole amongst each of our patches of shoots and we fidgeted as
plants began winding their way up. My brother noticed flowers
first, orange bursts which soon blossomed and stuck out their
runner-bean tongues at us.

We stuck our tongues out too.

My brother began to pick and crunch. I huffed. Mum said *some
things take more time, Hollie* as I wracked my brain for what I had
done wrong. Not one flower. I watered; waited some more. Then
one morning, my brother squealed, raced into my bedroom,
grabbed my hand and ran me excitedly outside. From nothing,
my plant had very mysteriously sprouted twenty, if not more,
identical and gigantic runner beans over night

I didn't question it

just stared – held my brother's hand
beaming with delight

i hadn't seen you in your nightie, mum
sneaking out in moonbeams, clutching
torch, bought beans and sewing kit

i didn't see the threads at first
green, camouflaged
meticulous, your running stitch

i didn't see your slippers soiled;
back hunched, weary
in that tricky light

just stood with my big brother
held his hand tight;
loving life

LOVE!

(written aged 9)

*I got given a big sheet of stickers one day when I was nine.
One of the stickers was of two parrots staring at each other with
a glittery red love-heart between them. The parrots were lined thickly
in bright sparkling gold. I felt straight away it was the most magical
sticker I had ever been given. I wrote a poem for my mum and dad
and nervously titled it 'LOVE!'. I remember feeling very grown-up
and carefully sticking the parrot sticker to the left of the title to mark
how serious I was about this. I thought the line 'love is the poor man
selling the beer' was really cool. I had never seen an old man selling
beer. I still haven't. I don't know if it even exists as a job. But I liked
that line a lot back then because it had alcohol in it, something I
knew I wasn't really meant to talk about. After writing the last line,
I immediately chickened out of giving it to mum or dad. I put it into
a maroon folder and hid it under my bed, feeling embarrassed I'd
written it and petrified someone would find it. A few days later I
moved it into a separate 'secret' pocket at the back of the folder.*

Love is the moonlight shining clear gold,
Love is the beauty you cannot hold,
Love is the flower that shines on your face,
Love is silk and love is lace,
Love is the ship sailing on by,
Love is the sunset that brightens the sky,
Love is the birds that nest in the trees,
Love is the soft, whispery breeze,

Love is the fire bringing warmth to your heart,
Love is the people that will never part,
Love is the oak tree, standing alone,
Love is the pebble, love is the stone,
Love is the animals all over the world,
Love is the star, silvery pearled,
Love is the beauty in which I seek,
Love is the old man, poor and weak,
Love is the wind blowing around,
Love is the grass on the ground,
Love is the river, shallow and clear,
Love is the poor man selling the beer,
Love is the rain, love is the snow,
Love is the one thing that will never go,
Love is the story you are told,
Love is the warmth, love is the cold,
Love is the torch leading the way,
Love is the thoughts you have every day,
Love is the sea, frothy and blue,
Please believe me, I love you.

God

(written aged 10)

After the first Christmas Eve midnight mass I remember

God is all forgiving.
He only wishes well.
But if he doesn't like you
I'm afraid you burn in hell.

MIDNIGHT MASS

(written aged 30)

i still remember the look he handed me with the bread

said *those who do not eat it*
                    will go to hell

said *those who do not believe*
                    will go to hell

said *those who eat it for false reasons*
                    will go to hell

i wondered   sitting sweating
what was worse –

knowing i was going
– or showing everybody else

[8]

TRAP

the woods were dressed in autumn
we were eight and nine and twelve and ten

we dug a hole to catch the grown-ups in!
(criss-crossed twigs, laid leaves on top)
we hid, spying from our holly den

we dug a hole to catch the grown-ups in!
the dog fell in; broke her leg

silently we hung our heads
— headed slowly home

the crunch of each leaf underfoot
now clear as cracking bone

A lad I was 'seeing' at school called me an ice queen when I was about thirteen. Not viciously, just a defensive shun after, I think, I either pulled out of snogging while walking awkwardly holding hands round the netball court at break – or didn't want to get fingered at the house party/bowling alley/quasar centre. Something like that, I can't remember the exact event. All I know is that I took it on board far too deeply and for years afterwards wrote poems comparing myself to cold things or things that needed to defrost, then later, poems about how love had finally melted me.

Cold

(written aged 13)

I am an ice cube,
I am new lying snow,
I fall into my angel
And I'm never gonna go.

I'm winter waters,
Below the frozen lake,
I'm hail and I'm sleet.
I am the first snowflake.

I am a tub of ice cream
Waiting frosty to be sold.
I am a carving chipped from ice.

Basically, I'm cold.

Ice

(written aged 14)

I am an ice cube waiting to melt
My coldness will thaw
As I fall to the floor
And my softening trickles be felt.
I'm a flower waiting to be smelt.

extract from And Now He's Going to College

(written aged 17)

Now he's going, thinks he knows me
Wasted time, never unfroze me
Never felt the willing heat from me
Can't melt impossibility
Never felt. Frosted eyes can melt
Stomach sick and sore
I long to thaw the rest

AN UNNECESSARY CUP SIZE

One of my strongest memories of early secondary school was in Year 7, sobbing silently in the girls' loos as I tried on a bra for the first time. I didn't want to ask my mum or any grown-up to take me shopping for one because I had no physical reason to wear one and I already had some crop tops. I wrote to my cousin Tracy instead. She sent me a parcel down from Glasgow with an old bra of hers. I remember it more vividly than any other item of clothing I've had: a proper bra with a proper pingable bra strap, white cotton, a tiny metal clip on the back and small pinky-red strawberries printed all over it. I never thanked Tracy as much as I wanted to. I took it into school with me to try it on. I've never felt as strange in my skin as that day. Perhaps pregnancy, but at least I could talk about that more openly and had lots of complimentary support. Morphing into an adult's body feels so odd. I tried to capture it here, but I can't.

i hoped that my embarrassment would dissolve into grown-up-ness
instead i stood all lunch break long – examining this fledgling flesh

in the blessed space of cubicles – oh sacred locks allowed in school!
– girls' loos, shirt off, muffled sobs   *what a stupid fool*

my backbone pinched so many times, as schoolboy flirting searched our shirts
i did not *need* a bra yet. fact. chest flatter than the misread earth

i rubbed the stretchy straps between my fingertips in slight disgust
unclipped the metal clip   slipped it on   clipped the clip back up

unclipped the clip again as fast   screwed it up   clenched the ball
teardrops licked   mascara fixed   i strolled across the hall to class

translucent shirt-back faced the lads   absorbed their eyes   i stared ahead
tried to solve the fractions   nipples palpable as pencil lead

because i want a strap for boys to ping was no reason for a first bra trip
i shut my bedroom door that night   waited for the hall to dim

silence   mirror   bedside lamp
clip   unclip   clip   unclip   clip

MACARENA

the lips we opened at the school discos tasted of sweeties
as tongues slipped in uncomfortably
manoeuvring saliva around each other's throats
pushed too deep inside, at times, we gagged

music-tempo-shift-signals-mid-school-disco-slow-dance

now little boys recoil to
line the edges of the room
– a centrifugal dread
the girls – darted to the loos –
eventually sneak back

half the track now passed
vomit rising just below a gag
as the mini men now ask
the mini women for a dance

some nervous laughs
till timid arms
touch behind each other's backs

kangol flat caps now flipped back
kappa caps like finishing-school books
balance high on curtained heads

'I'm gorgeous' gold logo tops
stretch across girls' chests
attempt at sexiness

short boys dance with left ear pressed on taller girls' 'breasts'
shorter girls use taller boys' shoulders as chin rests
boys and girls not dancing, watch. mock. deny distress
oversized US basketball vests almost reach the boys' ankles

feet piddle round
in pathetic, clumsy, magnificent, circles
to east 17's best lullaby

brian harvey *may* be a skank, we'd concede,
but tony mortimer is a piano *genius*

two minutes
torment
bliss

before the macarena kicks in

lines of us now grinning
follow suzanne
changing moves from
two hip-holds
and a half-turn jump
to two pats of our crotch
and a fake lick of our palms
to mimic cunnilingus

we giggle consciously; the boys stare
none of us knowing how it actually goes down
down there

then we race to the tuck shop;
um bongo and gummy bears

ON BEING A TEENAGE GIRL IN
THE COUNTRYSIDE

waiting was the worst

mud on our shoes – scuffed
arm to arm – elbows interlocked
as we lined up at the far edge
of the furthest field
like a flimsy hawthorn hedgerow

we'd seen that tractor
yielding pace from danni's garden
we raced the public byway path
turnstiles turned
scaled the padlocked gates
our smiles and panted laughter
fading into nervous breaths
as the speck on the horizon widened
panicking in case he caught us
before everybody was ready to

go!

trousers then pants pulled low
as fourteen fourteen-year-old arses
signalled flesh across the field

then

         sprinting
    back
            to danni's house
before

    he had a chance

       to tell us off

looking back now
he probably liked it quite a lot

YANKING

For a very good friend still!

apparently
'up and down'
did not mean
like a lever
like a door handle
like a joystick
like a casino slot machine

it meant
up and down
fingers curved around
gentle strokes from shaft to tip

we only learnt this
after she had tried
the alternative
yanking motion
and almost snapped
her boyfriend's dick

we gathered; listened
stroked her back
our impulse-perfumed shirts

we stroked her back
in hidden prayer:
thank fuck
she did it first

MR KENT

we bought our teacher
pants that said
'you're horny'

he opened them
on monday morning
blushing
like a boy our age

three fifteens
versus thirty five

less confident than us:
us watching him in sobs

pants that said
'we think you're horny'

– cos we thought we thought he was

TRAINING DAY AT BOOTS THE CHEMIST

the last part of the training day was best –
three school friends for a sunday job in boots

we'd been through
health and safety
canteen procedure
warehouse refill
shelf stacking

now we had to crack our reaction to customers
who bought 'embarrassing personal items'

rowena and me stormed the aisles for

condoms!
curry flavoured!
smooth and rippled!
extra large! for
tampax packs!
verruca pads!
tena towels!
fungal creams!

watching becky cut her eyes at us and squeam
as the manager helped her beep them through the till

revenge came my first working week
when miss strolled in and
            confident
        unashamedly
bought a fifty-pack of extra durables from me

i gaped and beeped
confused   and beeped
red-faced   and beeped

stammering to ask my teacher
if she had an advantage card
for those rubbers
and two clearblue baby tests

becky, next till
pissed herself

i'm still stunned miss didn't go to someone else's till instead

UNLIKE THE LADS

there were three types of virginity loss
we girls would chat about at school

sex while sober   which often came years after
sex while drunk   though both of those still years before
sex that helped us cum

ORGASM

but how do you tell if you've had one?
we'd ask
our friend who knew it all:

– oh you just know
she'd reply with a smile
– you *just know*

at the time
it was the single
least helpful piece of advice

later, we all realised
she was right

extract from PMT

(written aged 16)

The light-green colour of my friend Maddy's face when she got her period each month at school will remain forever in my memory. As will the fact she had to do her GCSEs in 'solitary confinement', as we called it, because of the pains and fainting. The summer term I wrote this poem, we were finally allowed to wear cycling shorts rather than gym pants for athletics; pants so small that sanitary towels had been easily identifiable at the edges and of course if leaking. The first time we started learning about periods was in GSCE Biology. One of my friends rolled his eyes in the first lesson and asked, whining, why we had to do this. When the lesson started and the teacher mentioned blood, he sat bolt upright and said, 'Oh my god, you bleed?' The entire lesson was swept away with giggling.

You can skip and wear pink and say 'ooh' as you twirl
What a fucking great laugh it is being a girl!

Each month without fail you get spotty and swollen
And you worry all day that a red blotch is showing

And you cramp into class and you have to act fine
And in PE you stress that it shows at the side

Those nappy-like pads in those fucking gym pants
Maddy's fainted again, how's she coping with that?

And your stomach blows up like a bloody balloon
And you're just feeling bloated and know that real soon

People will notice and people will stare
And people will laugh and no one will care . . .

extract from Naked Insecurities

(written aged 17)

I wrote a lot of poems like this at this age. They were all very long!

. . . Blind eyes turn around
In my head I'm dancing and laughing and smile
DeaF EARS hear me crying. You stand by my bed.
I lay back my neck.
Tilt my head at the chequered sky, closed eyes of mine
Relax

While I imagine you
Imagine me
With us.

Alone I'm dreaming, unawarely screaming, nowhere near.

Until you appear. It clears my head.
Imagination still exists. Confidence is dead . . .

Blonde Jokes

(written aged 17)

Scribbled angrily on a Little Chef break. I hadn't actually spat in anyone's food then, just annoyed by a few customers, it seems

I know this might not sound like much but every time I wake up, wear a skirt, a dress or put on a tiny bit of make-up, it's taken up by those who wanna shout. Girls who wanna let some hatred out, guys who wanna get their dick out – it's made into a focal point, forcing a front and token from me, boy it stresses me, won't let me be, like the colour of my hair's got fuck to do with me.

I know this might not seem like much, a touch of aggro but you don't know what I go through, you don't know the lines I flow through every day. So disarm me, laugh at me, alarm me, but I am sick of being fucking called a barbie, when I have nothing stuck or hanging on my body to suggest that I am open to caressing with breasts that can be dressed in whatever clothes you want. I am not a fucking doll so please don't treat me like dumb because I'm blonde.

It's a patronising world I've been living in, I'm guillotined and livid, been a teen but never given in but this given image sticks and I am fucked to death of all those stupid pricks. Cos I am sick of sitting there smiling while some man stands back undermining me, making blonde jokes and thinking that's all fine with me, just a pretty little thing, little blonde and thin and then it's fine for he

to tease me please I'm on my knees and begging you, cos while
I'm smiling sweetly I'm just thinking how to deaden you.

17, waitress in a little chef café and I've never seen so many grown
men who should be put in nappies, so slap me please I need to
wake up. Cos you seem so fucking foolish and rude that you see, I
don't believe in that, but please believe that I just spat in your
number seven burger and salty chips. Cos when I'm made for days
to serve food to idiots, smile to lip-licking twits, I tell you I'm
losing my wits. Sitting opening your thighs and grabbing your
crotch, telling me there's a hole in your trousers and you want
blondie to sew it up – and you expect me not to grow up thinking
what the fuck, you expect me not to throw up in your face or
just to mop it all up, just a little blondie thing, belittling,
I spit on the whole damn thing.

Cos I am sick of hearing jokes about the blonde.
Small tits and something's wrong, some wits but nothing strong
girl. I swear it's true. The day I cook again for men like you,
I'll use your balls to make the stew.
Trust me, I love lots of men but I do not like all of you.
I am so fucking bored of you
and your dumb blonde jokes.

NUMBER SEVEN
SEVENTH HEAVEN BURGER

he joked
he'd fire me
if i didn't spit

staring into the open burger bun
a flimsy slab of pale meat ready on the left side
watered-down ketchup squirted to the right
slightly browning lettuce laid, and
cucumber slices cut too thin
both quietly soggying the dough

he watched me – 'management control' –
my dry mouth trying desperately
to scour cheeks for dregs
a few collected drops of dribble
dripped between my gritted teeth

he joked
he'd fire me if i didn't spit

i felt that
sticky bubble
drip from seventeen-year-old lips
onto the greasy burger meat

plated up

i served the number seven
seventh heaven burger
with a side of chips and peas

to the man
who never let her speak in front of me
said she couldn't *have the fucking pie*
told the *bitch* to *know her fucking place*
every time i took their order
at the motorway café

ESCAPING THE BULLIES

and you just kept on drawing dragons
as the classroom mocked your name
as if the focus on your pencil sketch
could scrape the taunts away

and you just kept on drawing dragons
and i watched each scale sketched in
your teardrops splash   a little smudge
each sharpened shape of each new wing

and you just kept on drawing dragons
and your dragons looked enraged
and i willed through every lesson
for your dragons to escape the page

and you just kept on drawing dragons
and i felt their flaming breath
and you leapt onto the wildest one
and yelled out 'go and fuck yourselves!'

and you just kept on drawing dragons
and your dragons beat their mighty wings
and you rode – crash! – through the classroom roof
and the classroom roof came caving in

and you just kept on drawing dragons
and i watched you tear away
your sky sketched red in years of rage
your middle finger raised

and you just kept on drawing dragons
and your drawings were so bloody good
i told you once and smiled a bit
– but that was all i ever did

WORKING IN THE PHOTO DEPARTMENT
AT BOOTS THE CHEMIST

when the rota said 'photo'
      relief
'cookshop' was grim

second floor
one till
on your own
all day

three customers
in six sodding hours
sometimes, still
you could not move
from that till
must look busy, hollie
look busy
hollie   head up   look busy!
hollie!   head up!
look busy
giving not one shit
i had   no   fucking   idea
what those
brita filters did

the photo department was so much better; instead of selling kettles

those sundays were spent expectant, as the
negatives came to life on the conveyor belt
no customers on sundays see
just memories, printed in reverse order
we watched them reborn

> (willies were the best, of course
> close-up ones or sex shots)

quietly, we'd discuss which photograph
to place on top in the paper wallet
for the people working weekdays
– imagined maureen – monday morning – cheeks aflame –
as she made her way through the correct customer procedure:

1. Greet the customer.
2. Ask the customer's surname.
3. Collect the customer's photo wallet.
4. Open the photo wallet and show the customer the top photograph.
5. Verify whether this is in fact their photograph.
6. Take the payment.
7. Thank the customer.

that sunday, a crowd had gathered round to see the dress
(wedding photos attracted almost as many staff voyeurs as sex)
and she looked stunning   *gorgeous bride!*   *how lovely!*
staff revived, all smiling

> (well, a cock shot always shocked
> but this timing was atrocious)

we questioned it at first
erupted more with each exposure
– the photographs were always printed in reverse order

it went:

                                    the wedding night
                                    the groom arrives
                                    the bridesmaids
                                    get their make-up done

                              the groom. a tongue
                              some breasts. dark sky
                              mouth giving head
                              lips not his wife's

                        a taxi ride
                        his hand inside
                        her opened thighs
                        some blurry gropes

            more shots
         first round
the stags leave home

the bride collected first thing monday
like a kid come to a sweetie shop

i still worry that we should've put a different photograph on top

NO BALL GAMES

*'police and local authorities have given their backing to a gadget
nicknamed mosquito that sends out an ultra high-pitched noise that
can be heard only by those under 20 and is so distressing it forces
them to clutch their ears . . . eventually they have to move on'*
– Telegraph

*'It's been said that adults spend the first two years of their children's
lives trying to make them walk and talk, and the next sixteen years
trying to get them to sit down and shut up'*
– Dav Pilkey, Captain Underpants

there are no
welcome signs
no signs of life
at night the signs
reflect the fight

'NO ENTRY' here
'NO UNDER-AGE'
no music bars
no clubs, no raves

like ghosts
the 'youth' now shuffle round
youth clubs closed
for lack of pounds

some kids dine
in heated homes
playrooms full of
friends and phones

others roam
for empty parks
homes too small
or simply can't

not allowed
to bring friends back
no owned space
to sit and chat

groups of friends in parks
now *gangs*
hanging out now classed as
hatching plans

I think the hardest age is teen
too old to play, too young to wander free
by night 'NO UNDER 21s' inside
by day no play 'NO BALL GAMES' signs

no throwing, catching, football matches
one broken window, council snatches
every patch of makeshift pitch
not got a garden? give a shit!

that small green patch is yours no more!
'NO BALL GAMES' signs stuck in their hordes

in parks, these signs all laugh the same
'NO OVER 14s' – *please go away!*
no roundabouts, no swings, no slides
you'll drink, you'll shag, you'll sit outside!

where teens ride roads, now metal poles
pop up in formal demon drones
'NO SKATEBOARDING', no wheels, no bikes
all public concrete set with spikes

still headlines cry – obesity!
– computer games! – too much tv!
'KEEP OFF THE GRASS'
'KEEP OFF' 'KEEP OUT'
'NO BALL GAMES' here
no teens allowed

so now
boredom
stinks of shit

from sewers, seeps to streets to poison kids
preaching, it lies in gutters lined in teenage kicks
deflated footballs, mud and teenage sick

with stomachs thick and sagging centres
minds left numb and fun repented
it snatches fire-filled beating teenage hearts
pours water over bursting teenage sparks

till nothing's left, nothing to do
towns now turned to teenage zoos
caged and locked, their pathways blocked
left only cock or trudging shops

as the young poor wait and rot
labelled yobs by headline cops

while adults frown
and walk away
looking down
on *youth today*

as children play
now let us pray

Politicians

(written aged 18)

*My dad used to force me to watch the news for five minutes before
I could flick to the brilliant six o'clock US TV I longed for:* Fresh
Prince, Blossom, The Simpsons. *It annoyed me no end. I used to
moan about what was the point in forcing me to watch this stuff until
I could actually understand what the hell they were talking about.
Every time I didn't understand their vocabulary, it made me more
annoyed. As did their accents. My mum warned me not to become
an inverted snob, probably one of the most important and difficult
lessons I've tried to learn. When I wrote this poem, I'd been forced
to watch politicians speaking on the TV again by my dad when
I was desperate not to miss the start of* The Simpsons.

Hear hear, ra ra ra
Jolly jolly, fa fa fa
Yes yes, no no,
First speaker – you may go

Bla bla bla, I'm such a toff
Ya ya, cough cough
Fa fa fa, I'm very rich
Jolly jolly, twitch twitch

Bla bla bla 'A better year'
Knock knock 'hear hear'
Fa fa fa 'turn things around'
Clap clap. Sit down

Clap clap. Next one on
Bla bla. He's wrong
Fa fa fa pause pause
'I'm right'. Big applause

Bla bla I've got 6 cars
Jolly jolly fa fa
Pause pause. Wait wait
Cough cough. Kids are great

Bla bla big applause
Fa fa 'better laws'
'Hear hear' bench taps
Sit down. Clap clap

Next one up 'I don't agree'
Ra ra 'Vote for me'
Bla bla 'cos I can'
bang my fists down like a man

Ya ya well I can lean
Ra ra to make it seem
like what I say is really good
Clap clap. Tap the wood

I wave my hand up in the air
to make it look like you should care
or point my finger round instead
to give some worth to what I've said

Bla bla 'I see I see'
Good Lord! In fact, you're just like me
You're dull, you're grey, you're almost dead
You never did those things you said

You 'want us equal, want fair rules'
and send your kids to public schools
you moan about 'the country's state'
books for schools, the time you wait

in hospitals, the lack of care
although *you* don't get treated there
you promise them you have a plan
but you've stretched the budget all you can

'There's no more money left' you say
'Except all that, but that's my pay'
'Jolly show, I'm just like you
– are you a politician too?'

extract from Désirs

(written aged 18)

From quite a young age, I was pretty obsessed with learning French. I went on the school French exchange when I was fifteen and discovered a world of teenagers who all rode mopeds, who drank wine in sips without puking it up afterwards and who listened to bands like Louise Attaque. I wanted more. I discovered a rapper called MC Solaar and would continuously replay a song called 't'inquiète' when it got to the lines 'quand j'atteins l'objectif je flanche / car je pense à tes hanches' (when I reach my goal, I flounder because I think of your hips). His voice was like audio porn. I started 'coding' many of my many terrible teenage love poems by writing them in bad French, so none of my friends or family (except Mum) would understand them if they found them. I would say they are some of the worst poems I have ever written.

. . . Je l'aime mais je peux pas
Encore. Encore la même.

J'fais pas des choses
qui te feraient mal au coeur
même si je les veux.
Comme j'ai les désirs! . . .

(. . . I love but I can't
Again. Again the same.

I don't do things
that would be bad for your heart
even if I want them.
Oh, what desires I have!)

POLITE

it was weird
being on your knees
when you didn't want to

not forced
but not really
free choice, is it (?)
when you think
you better just do it
and he's your boyfriend
and you wanted that
and no one's told you otherwise
and you're just trying to be nice
and he's just trying to be liked
and you're just trying to be polite
really, and you don't really mind
but you don't *really* want it
in your mouth
that much

lips open
larger than a
standard spoonful
hair covering face
to avoid the gaze
he might notice
your mouth is down at the edges

as if you're watching a film
that someone else chose
and you're not enjoying it that much
but you're not really bothered
as long as there's popcorn
salty not sweet;   and no one gets hurt

thinking of other things now

your jaw's a bit locked now

just wanting him to finish really

so you can snog again

TEAMMATES

as we sprinted to the spare room
shut the door behind us
the party downstairs locked out
bottle back and forth in darkness

both players in the tennis team
I checked her steady-handed grip
and listened as she demonstrated
how to better relish it

like this? i said
racket handle stuffed in mouth
like over-eager cheesy chips
my seamless backhand useless now
my forecourt volleys never missed

as footsteps bolted up the stairs
fuck!

into the next room's
vacant bed

then
backs now pressed against the door
we chatted sport again

SAFE SEX EDUCATION

eyes avoiding the pupils' grins, he held the carrot up
rolled the gluey condom down; we copied, mostly failed
one ripped. lesson finished. be safe, he mumbled

six packs of condoms in your jeans' back pocket
you had already scaled the school wall together under darkness
reached the skylight we looked up to from maths class

glass shards and broken bottles scattered
across the roof, you clambered, holding hands with him
intent on this location

we decided the first time had to be exciting too
– a private competition between friends

me, years later, 1 a.m., condom packs wrapped
in two airtight plastic bags to save the rubber from the waves
we waited for the moon to pull the sea safely back
enough for us to swim round to the cove

rocks scaled, we lay, watched the sun awaken afterwards;
me not really understanding anything he said
but my French still getting better all the same

you two are married now
i lost his number the next month
we always listened well in class
you still think you won

HOT DOGS

the *special sauce, two euros more,* was ketchup mixed with mayonnaise
the tourists asked for 'frites' with that; the one french word they dared to say

i spent that summer stuffing frankfurters into eight-inch cut baguettes
watching british tourists burn; necks, soles, cigarettes
in the poolside hot-dog hut i sat, ramming poles in softened dough
squirting mayonnaise inside then pushing meat in each filled hole

i tried to scrub the grease smell off each night before I held his hand
i tried not to think of stuffing hot dogs as we lay down on the sand

SIDE EFFECTS OF BEING TWENTY-ONE AND TOO EMBARASSED TO BUY A CONDOM OVER THE COUNTER FROM AN OLD MALE SHOPKEEPER IN FRANCE

'the common treatment for chlamydia is a course of antibiotics.
If taken correctly it is more than 95% effective. The course of
antibiotics can be either a single dose, or a longer course of up to two
weeks . . . occasionally, doxycycline can cause a skin rash if you are
exposed to too much sunlight (photosensitivity)'
                              – online guidance for chlamydia treatment

i got sunburnt in glasgow
the next month

sat outside in george's square
my freckled arms
my face and neck
a cup of tea
burnt red
after a little less
than five minutes
in the daylight

when friends suggested
we move inside
still surprised at my pale
inability to cope

with a slightly bright
but clouded
dulling
scottish sky
laughing
'bloody hell hollie,
it's hardly a fucking sun trap!'

no one glimpsed the
chlamydia tablets
cowering in
the bottom
of my
rucksack

VOLUNTEERING IN A CAMBRIDGE BOOKSHOP

For a manager I never made a complaint against

i felt
his palms
every time i climbed the stairs

a pile
of heavy books
weighing down my open arms

always me
who had to climb
he piled the books up very high

always me
who had to climb up
and down the wooden stairs all day

laden
with the
donations of stray

tattered
paperbacks
local professors
intellectuals and literary lovers donated

first edition
classics filling up
my arms as i climbed
the cambridge staircase
from stock-room up to shop
from stock-room up to shop again

behind me every step, his belly groping for my spine
        palms upon my arse – light push – *to help me on my way*
                knowing i had neither hands free nor the confidence

to cuff
his fucking face

Language Learning

(written aged 24)

You make my toes curl up in two languages
My heart pump across the Channel
And as the beat gets faster
The waves race after my thoughts
Flicking from London to Paris.

Cos when I think of you in English
My lips begin quivering a little bit
I begin giggling like a little kid
And when you ask me to go for a drink at the pub
After 3 years I still feel a little sick
I panic.
Matchstick legs that might buckle and break
As butterflies take flight
Fluttering up in my belly
My breaths get heavy
Every time you put your hand
In my hand
Smile at me
And kiss my cheek gently
I turn to jelly and ice cream

But when I think of you in French it's slightly different
My nervousness switches off as you transform from
'mon copain' to 'mon amant'. You're not funny or sweet

In French, it's like this heat-fuelled meat-treat physical thing
In French, non . . . je ne pense plus à toi comme drôle ou mignon . . . non
In French, je pense à tes hanches (your hips)
Tes jambes, your lips ton grand, your big, grand, big coeur
Je pense de tes cuisses
Tes boutons de soleil
Et je veux me bronzer sur la plage de ton body all day
I just wanna pull up a deckchair on your chest there
And laze. Sans jamais arrêter.

I imagine feeding you croissants sur la plage,
Just splashing, sipping a little wine
Slipping a little time just to stare
Into tes yeux brown eyes.

In English
I get embarrassed and prudish getting nude or talking dirty
But in French it's so damn easy for me de fantasiser
– Je peux dire ce que je veux à toi
et parce que tu ne comprends pas
Je peux dire les choses que
Je ne dirais point
En anglais

In French
I might ask if I could lay you down
Pour te deshabiller, te sucer
But in English I would never say strip or suck
In French, I might ask if we could baiser
But in English I'm too shy to even utter the word
f.u.c.k

[53]

So you see
You make my toes curl up in two languages
It's like I've got two men, two best friends
I've got this horny Paris lover
Hidden under my loving Luton boyfriend's bed
I've got two men
Deux hommes, deux sentiments, deux bites
Alors two tongues, two kicks
Two types of bliss

Best bit is
Right now
I'm learning Spanish

Beautiful

(written aged 25)

As friends sit once again chatting about how beautiful Victoria Beckham is
I wonder if they've ever stepped outside and looked at a flower, a tree
Or waves breaking on the ocean creeping slowly towards the beach

As friends sit once again chatting about
The beauty of Victoria Beckham's new surgery
Her chiselled cheekbones, her Slimfast trim
The powdered skin of expensive make-up
Surrounding her permanently lasered lip-lined glossy lips

How well, they say, they sit
The new pert plastic surgeon's bits
Of plastic lift beneath her biggened bits of breast tissue
How, they too, wish they could do that perfect pout
Practised a thousand times in a million different mirrors
I wonder what they mean by beautiful

As my friends discuss her beautiful leather Gucci boots
Her boobs, the food she doesn't eat to keep her figure beautifully lean
I wonder what they see by beautiful

I wonder if they've ever been beneath the stars
Or felt the warm hands of a best friend
Rub oil along their naked backs
Or eucalyptus scent onto their chest

When the bin behind their bed is cramped
With flu-fuelled tissues

They discuss her shoes, her beautiful glossy hair extensions
Her gorgeous Beckham palace, her leather bags, her million dollar
Diamanté jackets a million mothers, sisters, daughters long to have
So we can look as beautiful as this woman

And I wonder if they've ever kissed anyone
If they've ever looked directly at the sunset and sat till sunrise
Run wet through raindrops dripping seas from cloudy skies
If they've ever cried with pleasure or dried tears with their own fingertips
From someone else's eyes

As my friends sit once again chatting about how beautiful Victoria Beckham is
I wonder if they've ever stepped outside and looked at a flower
Or wiped the hatred from their own faces and looked in the mirror
At their own beautiful reflections

BECAUSE THAT'S WHAT YOU DO

she said

move in
have kids
get married

her face looks as resigned as
getting porridge on a saturday

i circus-train my voice to smile
overact excitement
pray the tiger does not feel the flames
leaping through the ring of fire

still, she is giggling down the aisle
as they kiss
make vows
i cry
we laugh

throw little bits of paper
(biodegradable:
won't harm the grass)

first dance

we watch
get drunk
great night

not sure they made it to the bed

because that's what you do, she said
because that's what you *do*, she said

WATCHING MISERABLE-LOOKING COUPLES IN THE SUPERMARKET

they don't seem to
like each other very much
and they stay together
and they're not in love
and they made their vows
and they said forever
and they smile at friends
and the flowers wither
and when spring comes back
they're still together
and they're still together
and they're getting older
and the passion's run
from warm to cold
and no one wants
to be alone
or make a fuss.

but they don't seem to
like each other very much
but it's good enough
and the grass gets cut
and he likes the pub
and she likes the peace
and every saturday

the car gets cleaned
and they laugh with friends
but not each other
and in the evening
they eat food together
and they bicker
and they check the weather
and they watch tv
and they sleep together
they don't sleep together
and they sleep together
and they made their vows
and they said forever
and no one wants to be alone
or make a fuss.

and they don't seem to
like each other very much
and they talk of touch
like they talk of chores
and they don't get up
to get the door
and they're often bored
and they lie in bed
but they both feel sick
at the thought of
someone else
touching the other
person's flesh

AFTER PARTY / AFTER BIRTH

(written aged 27)

where were the balloons?
where were the party poppers?
where was the human tunnel
holding hands above our heads?

where was the champagne popped
sprayed straight into our mouths?
where were the crowd claps quickening
as we stepped outside with her?

where were the well done badges
slapped onto our tops?
where were the banners painted gold?
where were the silver trays of vol-au-vents?

where were the speeches and the toasts?
where were the three cheers for us?
where were the stamps and the shouts
and the claps and the fuss?
where was the drum parade?
the brass band?
the trombones?
the tambourines?
the pom-poms?
the three-tiered cake?
the horse and cart?
the limousine?

i *know* it's not a wedding
but did you not see what we did?
do you not get how hard that was?
did no one see me push; him pull?
does no one smell our sweat, my blood?
does no one know how much that hurt?
you are all just walking round
as if it's one more day on earth!

where are the balloons?
where are the clapping, waving crowds?
a welcome to this planet sign?
a prosecco as we all step out?

just a well done would be nice
at least hand us both a fizzy drink
one balloon strapped to our fucking car
to acknowledge what this is

THOUGHTS WHILE WATCHING
A BABY GROW

you've changed, we say
as if an insult
as if accusing
as if some
cunning plan we hatch
as if our minds
were never meant to
follow in the same path
as our bodies
as our pregnant skins
as our cells reborn
as our wrinkling
as if our thoughts
ought to be fixed
within a flesh
of never-ending change

you've changed, we say

as if the film
we watched last week
as if the book we read
as if that conversation
as if that day
as if each day

should not affect our
armoured adult thoughts

you've changed
we pause
you're not the person I once knew

disappointed
pointing fingers
across nostalgic afternoons

ASPIRATION

After watching Grand Designs *on telly for the last time*

sarah and tim have moved from the city
from highly paid jobs to the country's fresh air
they've bought a big barn for a barn renovation
and the tv presenter has side-parted hair

and i stare at the screen and tim looks at sarah
and the tv presenter talks a bit more
and he calls them 'adventurous' and 'daring' and 'brave'
as twenty blurred workmen parquet their floor

and i stare at our walls and the picture-hook holes
and the mark on the carpet i couldn't scrub out
and i imagine fresh paint and wallpaper patterns
and affording thick curtains that trail to the ground

and tim's sitting down with the architect now
and he wants 'bigger windows to let in more light'
and sarah is showing off heavy silk fabric
that they haggled to five pounds in bali one night

and sarah and tim now sit sipping coffee
as the tv presenter tells them they're 'mad'
and they nibble on nuts from a vintage glass ashtray
as ten workmen sweat just in shot out the back

and i plump up the cushions and imagine new cushions
as we nibble on nuts eaten straight from the packet
and tim says 'sometimes i think I'm *too daring*'
and we see sarah's smile pat the arm of jim's jacket

and i imagine fresh paint and wallpaper patterns
and buying more cushions and silk-woven sheets
and i think how those nuts might taste from a bowl
on a dining-room table carved straight out of a tree

and i daydream the intakes of breath as i sit
and announce that the paintwork is farrow and ball
and i imagine the cheese for the toasties we're eating
is chopped on a reclaimed wood solid-oak board

and then i get bored of this dream
and i realise i do not like tim
and that soon enough
we die

DIVORCE PARTY

for a few friends
(if you ever get back together, please ignore this poem)

your divorce party was better than your wedding
nicer cake, less family fighting
and that guy we all secretly never liked
this time
was not invited

CALL ON ME

for all friends

we don't call on each other anymore
we all live too far away
and now impromptu visits worry you
might *interrupt my day*

you do not wake me up
on weekends
with screams pitched
to my bedroom glass

do not ring my doorbell
more than once
politer now
step off the mat

now we must *plan* to meet
in diaries
don't dance in pjs/
share the bed

you do not comb my hair
for hours, to practise plaits
– drink tea instead

I love you still, my friends
I count our meetings down like holidays
but dream each time the doorbell rings
it's you, *just called to play*

WHEN WE GOT TO THE BEACH

i screamed
sprinted to the sea
flung off shoes and socks
ran towards imagined heaving waves
and jumped each tiny trickle that I found there
with just the same excitement

you stayed back
took your socks off more timidly
giggled at your stupid mother
eventually took my hand

we jumped together
and we jumped together
and we jumped together

three hours later
collapsing on our backs
we made angels in the sand

the seaside always made me
want to scream

now
with you
i can

Rules for Turning Thirty

(written aged 29)

1. Do not giggle at comments or jokes you don't find in the least bit kind or funny. You don't need to try to impress everyone, Hollie. Loads of people don't like you already. You don't like people too. Deal with it.
2. If a business person has their briefcase on the seat next to them on the train stop moaning inside your head while standing for an hour – go and ask them to move it so you can sit down. You are an adult and should not be scared to do things like this anymore. They are probably not the horror you imagine them to be.
3. Wear what you want. Stop reading 'what to wear at thirty' advice.
4. Do not say *volvo* to your daughter because you still find it too difficult to say *vulva*. Seriously, come on.
5. Each time you are about to moan or criticise yourself while looking in the mirror, phone Gran instead. It is a much better use of your time.
6. Remember that not everyone gets to have grey hairs. Ever. It is a privilege you should not be moaning about. Dye it if you fancy. Just don't moan.
7. Make a will. It will not kill you or jinx your health like you worry it will.
8. Buy stamps and send lots of postcards to people.
9. Learn Spanish.
10. If you're not sure, that's OK.

OASIS

for my oldest friend

i am on tour
and you
you are following your husband in a hearse

i have to remind my daughter five times
that this is not a party, whispering
as she watches with your twin boys
the yellow balloons rising to the skies
their tail-strings floating out of reach

the crematorium is like a rock concert
oasis escapes the open doors, in the car park
crowds of tiptoeing school friends stretch eyes up
to catch a glimpse of the speeches inside

i can make it for the first hour
before love drops me at the station
and the train takes to norwich
where i will stand on stage
make jokes and read poems
to two hundred people
who have not bought tickets
to watch me cry
and do not need to know that

i am on tour
and you are following your best friend in a hearse

i regurgitate tales in robot tones
tell poems from an unknown throat
think of the photo of you
at my first birthday
your thick hair
bursting with bows and clips
think of the pain
as my mum pushed metal
into my near-bald
three-year-old skin
as i insisted
she decorate my hair like yours

i think of the place
we were both born
the village
we were both grown in
think of the day
we were both thrown out
of brownies together
think of the sofa
we ducked behind
as southgate tried
and missed
the day you cried
when i moved
you put your arms around me
i put my arms around you too

everyone says in unison
he was too young
he was too young
he was *too young*
as if in chant to bring him back
it doesn't work
my grandma furious
that she is still
alive and bored
watching more
children fall before her

the poems tumble out my mouth
like our learnt school lines
people seem to like it
i don't remember
just wondering
why i am here

and you
you have just followed your lover in a hearse

launched a yellow party into the air
to celebrate his birth

as our children now chase strings together
jumping throwing hopeful fists
grabbing for their suns

WHILE YOU CAN STILL DANCE

'I'm so glad I still dream. It's lovely. In my dreams I can still dance'

— my gaga

i try to imagine i'm you, gran
as you chat with me, tired in your chair
hands squeezing my hands as your hands always have
as you talk of your lifetime as blur

i try to imagine my feet are your feet
lifted to lessen the bloat
i try to imagine my breaths getting thinner
my thinning hair thickened by slight backward combs

i choose from your m&s cardigan rows
soften my hands with your cream
i try to imagine your mindset; the knowledge
that death is now surer than any new dream

my head on your shoulder, I listen
imagine your stories are mine;
that i run and i waltz in my dreams when i sleep
cos i no longer can in real life

now i try to remember i'm me, gran
still able to dance whenever I like
and when sad, I imagine your lips smack my cheeks
as if slapping me back into life

BIRTHDAY LETTER

the poorer you are
the sooner the queen should write

MIDSOMER MURDER

there's so much blood on the streets
why do we love to wade in it?
behind the safety of tv screens
we dip toes wet to the limits

it's the underside of life
we like to lick a little for some reason
obsess over lips, spill, red, kissing death
camera shots zoomed
into actors' faces screaming

we're dreaming this stuff into scripts every day
we get off on the gore
we say we love the petals and the perfume and the romance
but we are so obsessed with the thorns

our palms clasped tight round the stems
sure to make the red rose blush
our interest in murder disguised by a sweet-smelling scent
when it is someone else's lust

we don't want to be *real* victims
of course not
but we don't want to miss the best bits either
witness the crimson-stained drips spat in the gutters
where we seek out the drama

we find it thrilling, let's admit it
to watch distanced people bleed
as if seeing the bloodstained circles expand
reminds us our own sheets are clean?

lusting over shadows to stand in
where we can idolise the blame
we say we're into the detective
and the justice of the case
maybe a little bit ashamed

of our own grim fascination in this
in the details of the crimes
in the thorns piercing rose-red flesh
into other people's chalked outlines

it's a human obsession, perhaps
to look beyond the fairy-tale glory

but when roses are painfully laid
on real graves every day
why do we so love a murder story?

FAIRYTALES

don't end
they just finish on a high
like a sensible athlete
or a butterfly

RESOLUTION

I will not complain about another grey hair
not their absence of colour nor their violin strings

I will not complain about the way they proclaim themselves
their refusal to flatten or try to fit in

I will not spend any more time at this mirror
hunting new strands between finger and thumb

there is too much to do
and there are too many eulogies
spoken for those who had none

AND WE TALK

of healthy lifestyles
and we search the latest trends
and when children beg to play outside
we say: don't interrupt again

and we talk of superfood groups
and we talk of super strength
and when children beg to play outside
we say: don't interrupt again

and we talk about the tv show
we watched on better diets
and when children beg to play outside
we tell them to be quiet

and we talk about the seed packs
for handy fat-free snacking
and when children beg the park from us
we tell them we are chatting

and we talk about the 5:2
and the highs of cutting gluten
and when children pull our arms and plead
we tell them that is rudeness

and we pass round healthy lifestyles
from books piled up upon our shelves
and when children moan of boredom
we tell them: entertain yourselves

the children given up
now the evening's getting colder
we discuss the path to better health
warm dips now dent each sofa

DRESSED

i watch my daughter dress at weekends
her four-year-old wardrobe grab
she comes out of her bedroom
in a glittered dress and swimming cap
a pair of reindeer christmas tights
star sunglasses on her beaming face

i'm in a 'sensible' t-shirt and jeans again
i'm the caged one. *she* is sane

HICCUPS

you had hiccups after pasta
you asked me to frighten you

i told you:
WATER IS BEING PACKAGED
INTO PLASTIC BOTTLES EVERY DAY
WHICH IN THEIR MILLIONS ARE
TOSSED AWAY AND FLOATING
INTO FRIGHTENED SEAS
THAT FISHERMEN ARE FISHING THESE
INSTEAD OF FISHING DISEASED FISH

you said
that's not the type of fear
that helps get rid of hiccups

PLASTIC BOTTLES

*'The production of water bottles uses 17 million barrels of oil a
year and it takes three times the water to make the bottle as it does
to fill it'*

— Business Insider

there's not much
i find as pointless
as plastic bottles
filling shores

there's not much
for me that sums up
why less
is often more

than fresh water
wrapped in plastic
making money
sold and branded

there's not much
i find as pointless
as plastic bottles
filling shores

water packaged
then sold back to us
now polluting
its own source

BLOOD AND WATER

keep your closest safe and warm
until your dying day is done

i give my own kid twenty christmas gifts
ignore the kids with none

FROZEN

the party was manic

husband stood out back, demonstrably doing nothing. staring

as she ran around speeding
in a room of popped balloons
and *frozen* wrapping paper
ripped across the floor
kids cackled – ran riot
the cake – a half-sewn
frozen elsa barbie-doll
stuck in sweetened icing dress
she made that morning
we sang happy birthday
HAPPY BIRTHDAY! we sang
her daughter screamed
at the bigger piece of cake
her brother stole
she tried to tell him off
he laughed at her
the daughter ran
upstairs in tears
she yelled, she
offered us a tea
on double speed
sorry! i forgot, she said
sorry, would you like some? tea?

sugar? would you like some?
sorry! she said
nervous giggles

husband stood out back, fag in mouth,
demonstrably doing nothing. staring

as she tried to manage
a game of pass the parcel
too many kids
to stuff in to a circle
in a tiny living room
still a present fell out of
every single layer
of *frozen* wrapping paper
her eyes drifting
out the door
as they played
pin the nose on olaf
smile hollow
stance cold
as *frozen* blared
let it go again
from plastic *frozen* speakers
party food now served
upon on a *frozen* tablecloth
and *let it go*
and *frozen* cups
and turn away
and slam the door

and *frozen* plates
and i don't care
and *frozen* mugs
a raging storm
her red-eyed love
i put it down to tiredness
and a husband who made a point of doing nothing

I didn't ask her how she was
not once

the party was manic
she was manic too
three months later
the kids were taken
out of school

middle of the day

FINE

and she says 'hey, how u doing?'
and I smile 'fine' into the phone
if she'd skyped, I'd not have answered
cos then she would have known
that I am lying on my bedroom floor
a starfish on a rug
glass of wine, stinging eyes
desperate for a hug
that I worry I'm not coping
that I feel like throwing up
that I cannot keep up with my work
that I'm frightened when it's night

I ask her how *she's* doing
'oh,' she says, 'I'm fine'

VOLDEMORT

'Call him Voldemort, Harry. Always use the proper name for things.
Fear of a name increases fear of the thing itself'
                                              — Albus Dumbledore

'If there isn't a word you can easily use, there's a very big risk that
you don't use any word at all, and that's a problem . . . if there's one,
and only one, part of your body that hasn't got a name, then people
experience that as a taboo'
                        — Anna Kosztovics, on the Swedish 'snippa' initiative

i pick my kid up from pre-school
and i love to see her face
i love to see her face
as she runs to send a hug my way
as she runs to send a hug my way
same way as all the other kids

i pick my kid up from pre-school
and she begs to go and play
she begs to go and play
same play as all the other kids

one boy's hand is down his pants
his mother shakes her head, *my son*
fiddling with his willy since
the day he knew he had one!

and everybody laughs
and the kids play in the park
and everybody laughs

– *just like his dad then*
someone says

and everybody laughs

parents chat now, tales are told
of last week's supermarket trip
her three-year-old son shouted
my willy's hard mum – it feels so good!

and everybody laughs
and the kids play in the park
and everybody laughs

then the mother of a girl agrees
hands always down her pants
she jokes
and everyone is awkward
parents   slowly   filter   off

the doctor told my grandma
he would look at her *downstairs*
last week
          she went to grab her bag

the english language
perhaps the fullest in the world
over fifteen words for rain

everyone says willy
but no girls' word
is the same

she's been fiddling with her fanny (too rude)
she's been fiddling with her vulva (too grown)
she's been fiddling with her clit (oh no)
she's been fiddling with herself
since the day she knew how good it felt

he's been fiddling with his willy

she's been fiddling with her minny, with her ninny, with her minky,
with her mimsy, with her mimmi, with her mini, with her moo moo,
with her mooey, with her moo, with her doo doo, with her was was,
with her poom poom, with her gina, with her vee vee, with her foof,
with her foofoo, with her fan fan, with her foofadoof, with her floo,
with her floof, with her fuff, with her wee wee, with her wink, with
her wanny, with her boo boo, with her woo woo, with her hoo hah,
with her too too, with her nu nu, with her lul la, with her nunnie,
with her nook, with her twinkle, with her tuffet, with her fluffet, with
her muffin, with her janet, with her mary, with her mary jane, her
lulabelle, her cinderella, baby hole, her daisy, with her kipper, with
her kiki, with her tush, with her tuppy, with her pennie, with her
tuppence, with her twinkle, with her tufti, with her tulip, with her
yoni, with her flower, with her craddock, her fandango, her fandangle,
her fangeeta, her wizzie, with her front bum, with her fairy, with her
periwinkle, special place, her private parts, her girly parts, her lady
bits, her tiddlypop,
her plum

they've been fiddling with themselves
since the day they knew how good it felt

when will everybody laugh?
when the father of a girl agrees

just like her mum then!

when will everybody laugh?
as the kids play in the park

when will everybody laugh?
as the kids play in the park

NIPPLES

when did we start to dress mermaids in seashells
or force their hair forwards, long, to cover their breasts?
when did we start dressing mythical females
as they swam side by side, mermen's bare chests
still allowed to be brushed by the waters?

when did we start selling toddler bikini tops
for one-year-old daughters to cover child flesh?
when did we start drawing eve with three fig leaves
as venus de milo waits, nervous she's next?

when did we start causing parents' distress
babies fed under adult 'modesty' bibs?
when did we move from statues of breasts
spouting milk into fountains for paddling kids
into faulty comparisons to groping and piss?

I imagine my grandkids on trips to museums
browsing displays of our censorship past
glass cabinets full of breastfeeding covers
and kids' illustrations of mermaids in bras

I'll tell them the tales of how I sat with their mother
in toilets that stank as she drank in the dark

and they'll ask me again and they'll laugh
and they'll prance around the room and they'll laugh
as if displaying the jokes of some alien culture
as they mimic and mock at our past

baffled by us
no longer forced in disgust
at their own flesh and bones
at their own mothers' breasts
at their own fathers' chests
at babies on breasts
at nipples freed up
on hot sweaty days

and the statues
of goddesses
watering kids
(kids paddling naked
all nipples and skin)
will flow into town squares again

SWEAT

from Offside *the play*

when i play football
i sweat
blood rushes to the surface
face goes red

when i play football
i smell
sweat drips from my forehead
back of the knees
armpits as well

when i play football
my lips go dry
my thighs itch on the inside
hair sticks to my head

when i play football
i get dirt up my legs
and when i take off my boots
the stench is like egg –
rotten

when i play football, i sweat –
like a woman

LADY

for the Chatterleys

she touched the gard'ner in the chicken hut
and makes a gorgeous cup of tea
the leaves brewed to perfection
her knickers round her knees

*

she got chlamydia at nineteen
and straight-a gcses
she has a keen interest in oxbow lakes
and fingering at house parties

she loves to pick fresh summer figs
and sit on male friends' faces
her gran is in a care home now
she visits every weekday

with an ear ready to listen
and each morning's daily paper
she likes to read in bed at night
or lie with a vibrator

wrapped in bedsheets made of cotton
three speeds and clit massaging
she does a linen wash each sunday
loves a deep run bubble bath

sometimes she has two sugars
other days she's sweet enough
in summer she wears skin on show
in winter, duffle coats and gloves
and big, thick woolly cardies

*

and as the fancy-dress party
of each new day revolves
she will continue trying human
in all its many roles

COCOON

raincoat zipped to my chin
for the bike ride
to work

hair bunned at the back
to fit in the hood
helmet clipped – tight
   i am waterproof

now pace reaches peak
the pedals attacked
winter tries hard
but the sweat coats my back
until two minutes left
i let myself go
cycling slowed
to unzip my coat
jacket front free
helmet clipped from beneath
hood stripped from my forehead
hairband released
hair ruffled with hands
to cool in the wind
body to elements
airing my skin

at that moment
i open
and peel myself free

i feel as close
to a new butterfly
as i'll ever be

BEES

'flowers are just prostitutes for the bees'
                              —Withnail and I

consensual sex all day long in multicoloured flower beds
horniness in tune to a sunshine spread of pollen scent
fresh-air living, honey dripping, *wings as well as legs*
no wonder we're so horrid to these fuckers

DUCKS

just paddling about, aren't you?
i throw you grains, watching you
i'm staring at those ripples
wishing i could live like you
just waddling and splashing, ey
just paddling about
like you just don't give a fuck

then i think of gang rape
and ducklings stolen
out of line

and i think i need to stop
romanticising
animal life

DUNG BEETLES

i wish i was as strong as a dung beetle
i wish i was as nice as a dung beetle
clearing those huge piles of crap

i wish i was as useful as a dung beetle
few humans are more useful than a dung beetle
i try to remember that

MAN

why do they speak of
women and children in war
as if the life of a man is worth less;

just the bit they don't mention
on news report figures
of injured
or missing
or dead?

A DEAD PIG, I MEAN?

i watch your five-year-old brain grappling to understand
what adults see as *normal*
because you don't yet know exactly how
our social rules work

i read you the papers again today
told you how some say the prime minister
      the conservative one? you ask
      – i nod
put his knob
      – i say willy, of course –
into a dead pig's mouth
when he was younger

you stare at me, expression dropped, silent for a moment
wondering whether that is as unusual as it seems

you check the facts with me
      his willy, mum?
      in a pig's mouth, mum?
      a dead pig, mum, I mean?

you stare at me then to the air, your mind collating data
you investigate some more, clipboard, pen to paper
you question me again, ask, with the cutest curiosity

if it's better if the pig was dead?
if it was hard to get his willy out?
if i've ever put my fanny
in a dead pig's mouth?

not understanding if this new piece of news
is just a game you don't yet know about

like monopoly or scrabble
just something adults do
like using different knives and forks and spoons
when different people come to tea
like killing turkeys every christmas
like making posh food out of force-fed ducks
like watching horses run in circles
like shaving poodles into different shapes
like punching in somebody's head
when one group of men kicking balls
kick more balls in a net

we make dinner
change the subject
build a cave house
out of lego blocks

your dad comes back
he kisses you
asks you how your
school day was

you ignore the question
look at him
get the clipboard out

inquire if he's ever
put his willy
in a pig's mouth?

no.

or . . .
— a chicken's?
— or a sheep's?
you list farmyards'
worth of options

till it's clear from
the consistency
of negative
responses

that this is
not a standard
place for
any private part
to be

you correct yourself
check one last time

— a dead pig, dad, i mean?

SHRINKING

For the British Library celebration of Alice in Wonderland

For the waitress who served us in Wetherspoons

the clock ticks twelve
she clocks off at ten
the costume obviously makes her
feel like a dick

a cheap hairband
of fake blonde plaits
strapped to her head
white virgin popsocks
that slip off her knees
and high heels that click
as she walks

she is pouring our tea
with her eyes to the floor
a glance half raging
    half just embarrassed
as wetherspoon's airport bar
blesses this book
    with one overworked waitress
dressed poorly as an alice

the fabric of the petticoat
clings tight to her folds

as a customer jokes
how he'd *get in her hole*
the scoop of the pinafore
exposes her tits
in that purposeful play
between woman and kid
between virgin and whore
that our fancy-dress thrives on
and our dear british culture
still loves to deny
it adores

the costume was hanging
   on the staff door at work
   and though she'd asked not to wear it
it's hard to be heard
when your heartless old boss
   is a loud-mouthed bitch
who bites off your head
for the smallest of things

so she circuits
the workplace
   again and again
begging the time to speed up with each round

but in the heat of her boredom
   and beckoning orders
     the hands of the clocks
just keep slowing down

now the mad midday-rush
of stag dos and hens
    come for shots of dutch courage
before they board planes

and with each tipple of liquor
the belittling chorus
grows more and more raucous
till the wild party reigns

she serves them more shots – smashed
she sweeps up the spills
    as customers' confidence
soars with each sip

and as the beered beasts around her
grow bigger and louder
she shrinks
    and she shrinks
and she shrinks

soon the whole bar is whiffled
with dodos and chicks
cheshire-cat grins
    that chortle and quip
and the chips and the ketchup drips
soon make her sick
    and the claws of the gryphons
keep grabbing her bits
    how cheerfully the crocodiles open their jaws

gobbling up in their hordes little fishes
    she thinks
    and with each copper-coin tip
    with each pervy pissed wink
each wipe of missed piss
each toilet-shift tick
    with each open-lipped comment
    from another rude prick
with each cocky complaint
    with each new working day
    with each person who says
she should be grateful for this
    that anybody with work
    should be grateful for this

she shrinks
and she shrinks
and she shrinks
and she shrinks
and she shrinks
and she shrinks
and she shrinks

to that rodent height
that minimum-wage work
and a lack of real rights
    make it feel sometimes
impossible to grow back from

LITTLE THINGS

i remember that feeling
knowing that nothing
would be the same again
the pain lessening
but the responsibility
as your dad
placed you in my arms
a terrifying shock

i remember that feeling
that i had never really known
what freedom meant
until you fell asleep
until you went to feed
entirely dependent on my chest

i remember the hospital gown
the dry toast, the total tiredness
scared senseless
buried in the bundled blankets
they wrapped you in
you looked at us
eyes squinting at a world
too bright for you to make out still
and i admit
my stomach churned

a love mixed with
claustrophobic bouts
elation mixed with
fear, as your face faced
that first morning sun

years later now
years of being mum
years of night-time walks
and waking cries
of eyes so red, rose-tinted lies
of tantrum tales
and screaming dreams
of up-all-nights and work-all-days
of pre-planning every inch of every day
all decisions based on you

your name is there
in flashing lights
in everything we do

and i admit sometimes it's too much
i have locked myself in bathrooms
just to get some space away

you had to come to work with me today
and then i took you to the beach

you swept your feet without me seeing
wrote 'i love you mum' soft in the sand

you asked me if i liked it
licked the ice cream dripped upon your hand
and watched me melt as fast

it's those little things we do that hold my heart

PICKING PLUMS
in the park, we are gods;
my shoulders, your throne, our
backbones as tough as the trunks.
lifting you up gets harder each year
but feeling you grab for those small
globes of gold, of orange and purple
and pink plucked fresh between
twigs, gobbled licks on your lips
is as close to alive as i'll
get. the crumble
we plan
every
year
has
never
been
made,
a few saved for your dad
the rest line the bellies we clutch
filled with far too much autumn again.

slice a strawberry north to south
cut a melon down the middle
halve a passion fruit and lick it out
split a fig at ripest purple
pick a plum fresh from a tree
suck the flesh clean from the stone
then lie back on the ground
and feel the earth moan

*   *   *

'Grown-ups never understand anything by themselves,
and it is tiresome for children to be always
and forever explaining things to them'

— Antoine de Saint-Exupéry, The Little Prince

*   *   *

(written aged 8)

Meadows yellow, brown and green.
Rainbows in the sky.
No litter on the grass or fields.
Butterflies flutter by.
River water sparkly clean.
No pollution in the air.
That's how the world should be
So try to take more care.

(body)

i

head

i dream of travelling most nights

watch *a place in the sun*
and pretend that's my life

i still believe in santa claus
never opened my eyes
when footsteps came into the room

i remember faeries clearly
sneaking out of forest doors

my memory is flawed for sure, i know
and my daydreams still sometimes overflow
– thankfully –

because this thing upon my neck
has carried me to places
i have never been
made me dreams
placed me into fantasies
i cannot afford
and will probably never see
in one short life

ii

mouth

i've been saying this for bloody years! she cries
the government doesn't fucking listen!
i've been saying this for years! he yells
fucking pointless politicians!

i sometimes wonder if we realise
(in all our expert armchair wisdom)
that nobody can hear us
through the fucking television

iii

shoulders

my shoulders are fucking delicious
smeared with freckles, blodged
like dirty, speckled come-ons
jumpers always 'fall off' one
shoulder, flesh to show off
t-shirt tops near sacrilegious covers
of these perched, glowing, dappled, oval beauties!

i know i shouldn't boast about my body
but i am bored
of being bad to it
so fuck it
i will brag

my shoulders are *fucking delicious*
no one told me
it's just a fact

iv

breasts

i never made it past the second stage
in the biology textbook

a three-tiered
teenage demonstration of
'growing breasts'

pre-teen
to pubescent
to woman

the last chest a 'proper' bosom
— we'd all get there next

i'd taken it as fact

i'm thirty-three next year
they still don't look like that

v

belly

i tell myself
over and
over again
to be proud

look down!
that space was a house!
heated perfectly with blood and food
tubed through an open belly-button it grew!

but some days i still can't help staring
some days i still can't help frowning at the softness
testing it with pokes
slapping myself for feeling
that this lack of tighter muscles is still
— sometimes
— on tired days
bad

my belly raised a life
why can't i focus on that?

vi

vulva

my granny will not say *that word*
or name *that place* on pain of hell

my mother is a nurse
but finds it terrible to say as well

i forced it for my daughter, but
stuttered 'volvo' for at least two years

my daughter, dancing naked,
sings it jokingly for all to hear

no idea the length of time this took

vii

bottom

It slipped out like silk.
No pushing. Paper spotless.
The perfect ghost poo!

viii

feet

they told the kids you could *tell a catholic*
from the way they walked, dad said

　　– from the point of their feet
　　– from the bend of their knees

at school
he said he was told that
as fact

the catholic kids were probably told it too
that *protestant shoes clipped differently*

old handed-down stories we pass on to kids

i told my daughter that cinderella's feet were big
and that the sisters
wished theirs were large enough to fit
when the glass slipper was placed before the three

unfortunately
she's now learning to read